Jungles

by
David Orme

Thunderbolts

Jungles
by David Orme

Illustrated by Craig Ashforth

Published by Ransom Publishing Ltd.
Radley House, 8 St. Cross Road, Winchester, Hants. SO23 9HX, UK
www.ransom.co.uk

ISBN   978 178127 060 8
First published in 2013

Copyright © 2013 Ransom Publishing Ltd.

Illustrations copyright © 2013 Craig Ashforth
'Get the Facts' section - images copyright: cover, prelims, passim – dirk ercken, gbohne, ; pp 4/5 - Francisco Romero; pp 6/7 - Makemake, Cesar Paes Barreto; pp 8/9 - dirk ercken, http://veton.picq.fr, thobo, David Parsons, Cburnett; pp 10/11 - koles, Brocken Inaglory, PRA, Chris 73/Wikimedia Commons, Melanie Szirony; pp 12/13 - David Dennis, Paul Mannix, David Arvidsson, Marcus Lindström; pp 14/15 - Marco Neumayr, Mike Baird, Morkelsker, Geoff Gallice, Mr_Vector; pp 16/17 - browndogstudios, dusko matic, Mara Radeva, Debra Wiseberg; pp 18/19 - Marco Neumayr, Captain Herbert, Marcos Pereira, Greg Hume, William Scot; pp 20/21 - Aidenvironment, Diorit, browndogstudios; pp 22/23 - browndogstudios, Piyachok Thawornmat, Randi Ang, Amcaja, Marco Schmidt, g01xm; p 36 - lubasi.

A CIP catalogue record of this book is available from the British Library.

All rights reserved. No part of this publication may be reproduced, stored in a retrieval system, or transmitted, in any form or by any means, electronic, mechanical, photocopying, recording or otherwise, without the prior permission of the publishers.

The rights of David Orme to be identified as the author and of Craig Ashforth to be identified as the illustrator of this Work have been asserted by them in accordance with sections 77 and 78 of the Copyright, Design and Patents Act 1988.

page 5

page 25

Jungles: The Facts

27